SURVIVING JAIL AND REBUILDING YOUR LIFE

This book gives an amazing insight into a world unknown to most people. The author has experienced this. His story is compelling, and a must read for everybody, not just those caught up in or involved with the justice system. This book's story cries out for much needed help for the mentally ill, and for a complete overhaul of the prison system.

–MOTHER OF A SON (WITH A MENTAL HEALTH PROBLEM), WHO WAS INCARCERATED

As a fellow Celebrate Recovery attendee, we walked through weekly meetings together for 4 years sharing our deepest secrets in a structure of complete acceptance; prayed and discussed our individual 'walk' during the commute.

The author has been a powerful example to me of a man who has suffered, showed much courage, and through his new found faith "is a new creation" 2 Corinthians 5:17. An authentic man will write authentically.

–BOB

For those who have seen the show 'Undercover Boss', I've often wondered what the results would be if someone like a lawyer, judge, or police officer would go undercover into jail for at least six months. In this book Hilgers, through his personal experience brings to the forefront what it is like to go through the prison system. This book is a must read, and covers the experience from arrest, to jail, release and rebuilding one's life.

–FATHER OF A SON WHO SURVIVED JAIL, AND REBUILT HIS LIFE

'GOD IS THE SOURCE OF MY STRENGTH IN WHOM I TRUST
THEREFORE I WILL NOT FEAR'

SURVIVING JAIL AND REBUILDING YOUR LIFE

ARREST – SENTENCING – JAIL – RELEASE – PROBATION – REBUILDING YOUR LIFE

W.C. Hilgers

ISBN 978-0-9938213-7-0

Cataloguing-in-Publication Data available from Library
and Archives Canada.

CONTENTS

Acknowledgements

Surviving jail, writing this book and rebuilding my life would not have been possible without God, and the support and encouragement of the following wonderful people:

- My parents for their support, their unconditional love and their encouragement to write this guide

- My brother for his support

- My good friend who was the only friend who stood by my side, who supported me, and who was used by God to start opening my mind and heart to Him.

- The Christian men that I interacted with in the jails, and who introduced me to group Bible study

- 'Champion', an inmate at Penetanguishene who led me to Christ

- The Gideons and The Salvation Army for the Bibles and Christian literature they make available to inmates in jail

- The facilitators, staff and my fellow group participants in the program I took that mentors men who commit similar offences

- My physician for her care and for her key role in diagnosing and treating my Bipolar Disorder

- The men and women at the Celebrate Recovery program at my home Church, my sponsor, and my accountability partner – who all played important roles in my recovery journey

- The owners of the first company that hired – in spite of complete disclosure of my past, and when I was still on probation.

- My Brother in Christ for his friendship, and introducing me to Promise Keepers, a weekly Bible Study, and a volunteering role at a ministry providing meals for low income and homeless people

- My girlfriend, who loves me unconditionally

And most important of all, Jesus Christ, for saving and transforming me!

Introduction

At the age of 49, through the combination of a 40 year sexual addiction, a workaholic life style, mental breakdown, bipolar manic episodes and bad choices, I made a train wreck out of my life. The consequences included losing a marriage, forgoing any relationship with my three children, losing an executive job, losing my reputation, depletion of all my financial resources and assets, bankruptcy, losing all but one friend, a planned public exposure of my addiction and bad choices, arrest and conviction for a criminal offence, and sentencing to six months in jail and three years' probation.

I was not the only one who suffered painful and costly consequences. Others included my ex-wife, my children, my parents, my friends, my employer, and fellow employees at the time who had respected and looked up to me.

Other than speeding tickets I had never had any dealings with police or the criminal justice system. Starting with my being arrested my parents and I were completely green as to the shocking, confusing and very difficult world I was about to enter into. I was absolutely clueless as to how to navigate the system, how to stay safe during incarceration, what probation was, and how to rebuild my life after release.

This book is intended for individuals who have never been involved with the criminal justice system. Travelling through the criminal system is extremely stressful, confusing and difficult. Being processed at the jail(s) you are sent to is intimidating and depressing, and for me it was like entering a surreal world.

The purpose of this book is to give first time offenders some insight into what to expect from the time of arrest, through to incarceration and release. I have also provided suggestions on how to rebuild your life. It is my prayer that you, your family and loved ones will find this guide informative and helpful, and that it will help calm your fears and anxiety.

You will read in this guide that I became a born again Christian as a result of my experience. Without Jesus I would not be alive now, and I pray that God will guide and protect you as He did me.

To police officers, lawyers, judges, guards and probation officers who read this book: My purpose has never been to offend you, or to create any negative impressions about your profession. The comments expressed herein are based on my personal experience, and I recognize that they absolutely do not apply to the majority in your profession. You play a very important role in our society, and I recognize that clients/offenders, and the crimes that you deal with, can be very challenging, and in some instances dangerous. You also see and deal with the victims and consequences of crime. I sincerely appreciate and respect the important role you play in society.

The information provided in this book is based on my experience with the Ontario Provincial Justice System. I am certainly not an expert, but it is my hope and prayer that this book will be helpful to all who read it, and perhaps result in some positive changes.

ARRESTED

One Sunday afternoon the police showed up at my parents' house where I had been staying since I had blown up my life. They were plain clothes, driving an unmarked van. One was male and one female. They presented as very friendly and low key. They showed their badges, and said they just wanted to talk with me. My parents invited them in, but they said they wanted to go for a drive with me. When they drove around the corner from my parents' home they pulled over and arrested me (read charges and handcuffed me).

TIP: Do not invite or allow police into the place you are staying, or agree to leave with them, unless they have a warrant that you can read.

TIP: Have someone present with you while talking with the police.

TIP: If they have a warrant for your arrest tell them that you wish to call your lawyer, or, if you don't have one, "a lawyer".

TIP: Police being nice can be a tactic to let your guard down to get you talking, or to accede to their requests.

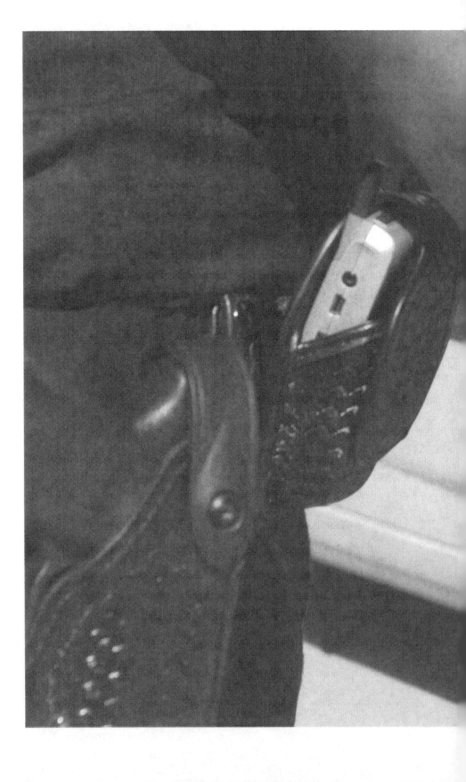

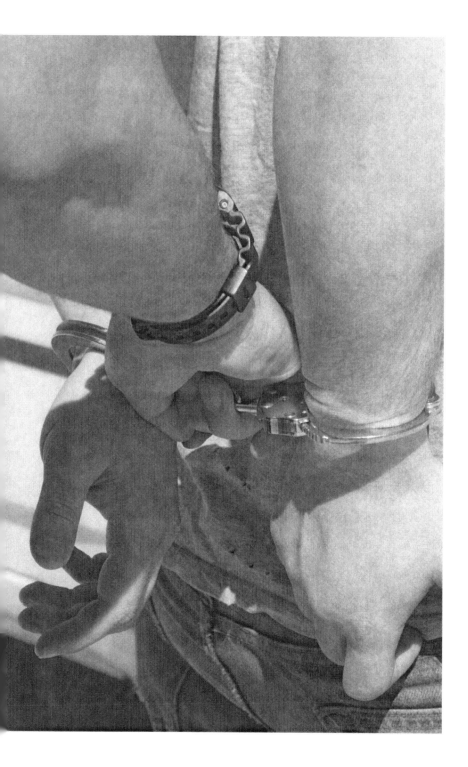

TIP: If you are on any medication, advise the arresting officer(s) of that, to ensure that it is brought to the police station.

TIP: If you are arrested and taken away, do not admit to anything. They may try to talk with you about something small or seemingly unrelated just to warm you up to talking. In my case they took the approach that they knew everything about my offence, and wanted to help me.

TIP: Ask where they are taking you, ideally in the presence of someone who cares about you.

TIP: If there is someone present when they arrest you, ask that person to call a lawyer.

TIP: If you know that you could be arrested at some point in the future, be proactive and find a lawyer that you, or someone you've asked to help, can get hold of quickly (as soon as possible, if you are arrested).

TIP: Remain calm, polite, do not argue or resist.

TIP: Expect to be shocked & afraid.

TIP: If you are arrested in your home, you will not be allowed to get any belongings.

TIP: Listen and remember what the charges are.

Police Interrogation

The officers drove back to my parents, to inform them of my arrest and ask for the daily medication I had told them I needed. Then they drove me to the police station.

I was brought to the basement of the police station into an interrogation room. I was in shock at the time, and don't remember all the details. They asked me if I had a lawyer that I wanted to call, to which I said no. They then put me on the phone to call a duty counsel lawyer. He said some things, but I didn't know what to do. I was in no mental or emotional shape to make informed decisions, let alone process what my situation was.

Then they placed me in a cell/interview room for what seemed like hours. They played good cop/bad cop, and came and went several times. They used leading and suggesting statements. I can see now that they were working to disarm me, wear me down, make me break down and confess in detail. I do not remember how long it went on.

I did not realize then that it was all being video recorded, and would later be used by the prosecution.

TIP: **Insist on a lawyer being present before you talk.**

TIP: **You do not have to answer their questions.**

TIP: Caution: They will likely start with seemingly 'normal' conversation, such as "I know you must be feeling bad now", or "Would you like a glass of water?" They want you to feel comfortable talking with them, and to believe that they are trying to help you.

TIP: Everything you say is being videotaped and can be used as evidence in your trial.

TIP: Note: My advice here is not to encourage you to lie, but to have a lawyer guide you to the best possible outcome for you and your family (and I am not overlooking any victims of crime).

TIP: Expect to be in shock, confused, scared, shaken, and feeling that your life over.

TIP: Be on guard for 'good cop, bad cop' tactics.

TIP: Ask for a glass of water, if they don't offer you one.

TIP: Don't feel like you need to answer their questions quickly. Think about your answer first.

TIP: If you do not have a lawyer their already, they will provide you with a list of lawyers. You will choose one and call them. Listen carefully what they say, and go with their advice.

After Interrogation

When the interrogation is done you will be taken where the holding cells (jail) are in the police station. You will be finger printed, then placed in a cell, pending your bail court appearance the next day. Being in jail the first time is scary, discouraging and depressing. When the jail door locks behind me I found it pretty hard not to lose it (especially with Bipolar). All the sights and sounds are like nothing you've experienced, and you may hear and see men in cells who are loud, angry, verbally abusive to guards, drunk, or high, etc.). I witnessed one man who wouldn't calm down and listen to the guards get his mattress and sheets confiscated. Then he was hosed down with water, and stayed like that for the night.

Likely you will spend the night in jail, and then appear in bail court the next day. If you don't have a lawyer, there are lawyers who are called 'Duty Counsel' who will explain what is happening and represent you at the bail hearing. You can find a Duty Counsel by asking around. You will want to call, or have called, whoever you want present at the bail hearing to support you and be your surety for bail if granted. If you haven't been able to call them, then your surety, loved one, or lawyer will have to call the police station to get the details of time and location.

The purpose of the bail hearing is to set the terms for

your release, if bail is granted by the judge. To be granted bail, someone has to be present and agree to be your surety. They also have to agree to the bail conditions; for example, that you have to reside with the surety, and can't go anywhere without the surety. There also will be a bail amount that your surety has to agree to and guarantee to pay in the event you break a bail condition. You will have to remain in the care of your surety, and abide by all bail conditions until the criminal trial moves forward. This could take from months to a year or more.

While you are out on bail you have to abide by the conditions or face additional charges. While on bail the justice system will slowly churn forward to the day of your sentencing trial. In many cases it can be months or even years before a case moves forward to trial.

Being granted bail is not a guarantee in every case. Depending on what the crime is, first time offenders are likely to be granted bail, if they have an approved surety.

TIP: **After interrogation expect to be fingerprinted and placed in a holding cell. It's an intimidating experience. It's a normal reaction to be scared and shaky as the harsh reality of your situation sinks in.**

TIP: **When you are brought to a courtroom for a bail hearing you will be assigned a duty counsel lawyer. Listen to him/her.**

TIP: **To be granted bail you will need someone to be your surety. Make sure it's someone you will be living with, and is prepared to guarantee that you will abide by the bail conditions.**

Finding the Right Lawyer

Selecting the right lawyer to take on your case can make a significant difference in what your conviction and sentence outcome will be. To find the right lawyer ask around, meet with a few, and don't feel pressured to make a quick decision on who to select. Try and find a lawyer with experience and a track record with your particular offense. Make sure you and your family, or a person who cares about you, feel comfortable that you could have a good working relationship with him/her.

Seeking out the 'best' lawyer can mean they will charge you the most, but that is not always the case. However, keep in mind that even having the most costly lawyer will not necessarily result in not getting convicted, or receiving the most lenient sentence. In my case, we were referred to the 'best' lawyer in Ontario with regard to the nature of my particular offense. We met with him at his office, and told him about the arrest and charge. His reply was, "You have nothing to worry about. You have come to the best lawyer to deal with those charges, and at the most you will get a weekend sentence, but it will cost you $85,000 in legal fees. The $85,000 made no difference in the sentencing outcome, and what we expected to be a weekend sentence turned out to be six months in jail. In hindsight, we made a poor choice.

The week before the sentencing hearing he called to say

he would not be there, that I didn't have to worry, and that one of his student lawyers would be present. The sentencing ended up being six months in jail, with onerous probation conditions. After the sentencing my parents asked the student lawyer for some time to ask questions. She said yes, and said she would be back shortly. She never returned.

If you have no income or financial resources to pay for a lawyer, then you may qualify for legal aid. With legal aid the government pays your legal costs. Not all lawyers accept legal aid clients because they get paid less.

TIP: **Discuss with your lawyer whether pleading guilty could result in more favourable sentencing terms, than if it went to court and you lost.**

TIP: **Consider that the longer the time it takes to get to the sentencing hearing, the more money it's going to cost.**

TIP: **A good lawyer does not mean the most expensive lawyer.**

TIP: **Take your time to select the lawyer who will represent you. Don't feel like you have to retain the first lawyer you speak with.**

TIP: **When you retain a lawyer be honest with them, so there are no surprises during your trial.**

The Legal Machine is No Respecter of Persons

The way the Ontario Provincial Justice System works, it doesn't care about your individual personal circumstances, such as whether you have a mental or physical illness, or what the impact to you and your family will be because of your arrest and sentencing. Get used to it. Once you're caught up in the system it's a different world than you're used to, and you have zero control or influence on it.

You will discover that there is a variance of sentencing lengths and conditions for charges/offences like yours. This is because judges have latitude with this, and the judge you end up getting can make a difference when it comes to length of sentence and severity of the terms and conditions (for example, length of probation, probation conditions).

Comparing your sentence to others with the same type of offense, instead of accepting the cards that you have been dealt, will get you nowhere, except angrier.

TIP: **Do not expect the Prosecution or Judge to take into consideration what the impact of a sentence (jail time, conditions) will have on you, your family, or employer, etc.**

Sentencing Trial

Getting to the point where there is an actual sentencing trial can take up to one or more years. Prior to the sentencing trial your defense lawyer and the prosecutor request and exchange information / evidence to see how strong their respective positions are. There can be a number of court room proceedings before the actual sentencing trial. It also can happen that you what is supposed to be the sentencing trial, gets delayed.

During the sentencing trial your lawyer and the prosecutor present evidence, and if witnesses are called then they go on the witness stand and are questioned. The trial can take a day or less, several days or much longer depending on the offence, complexity of evidence, number of witnesses, and experts etc.)

As a first timer in court you can expect to be intimidated and nervous. It is a cold, formal environment. Going to court looking presentable (clean, appropriate clothing), acting and talking respectfully makes an impression and can make a little difference in how harshly the judge deals with you.

Expect the prosecuting lawyer to talk about you, and to you like you are the scum of society, that everything she/he says is 100% correct, and that you need to be given the most severe sentence possible.

Sometimes your defense lawyer and the prosecuting

lawyer will discuss before the sentencing trial that in exchange for pleading guilty, the prosecution will agree to a less harsh ruling/sentence than what they would go for if you plead not guilty.

In addition to the length of jail time, the sentence will also include conditions. Examples include length of probation upon release, no weapons, no drugs or alcohol, staying away from certain people or locations.

TIP: Have some money in your pocket – minimum $50. This money will be placed in kind of a bank account for you at the jail(s) you will be in. What the money can be used for is explained later in this book.

TIP: Expect to be surprised that there will be many trial delays and postponements.

TIP: Expect your court appearances to be very intimidating.

TIP: During the sentencing trial you can take notes, and show your lawyer if you have any concerns or feel something the prosecutor presented as evidence is incorrect.

What Happens After You Are Sentenced

Once you are sentenced the courtroom officer will likely handcuff you, escort you out the back of the courtroom, and you will be either placed in a jail cell in that building, or taken back to the police station you came from. If you were out on bail pending sentencing then you will likely go to the original police station where the arrest proceedings took place, until you are transported to jail.

After the sentence verdict, you and your loved ones will not have an opportunity to speak with each other, or hug goodbye, etc.

The next step is waiting to be transported to the jail they are sending you to. In my case it was Maplehurst Correctional Facility in Milton, Ontario.

The population of those incarcerated at Maplehurst is a combination of those waiting to be sentenced (i.e. they were not granted bail), and those sentenced and waiting to be sent to wherever they will be serving their sentence. The waiting varies in length, as it depends on a place (cell) being available in the jail you are scheduled to go to. Most offenders transferred out of Maplehurst go to either the Penetanguishene Central North Correctional Centre in Penetanguishene, Ontario, or the Central East Correctional Centre in Lindsay, Ontario. These are both maximum security jails.

TIP: You are not allowed to bring any personal belongings (clothes, books or whatever) with you to jail.

TIP: If you are convicted and sentenced to jail expect that you and your loved ones will not be able to have contact or time to say goodbye. You will be handcuffed and led out through the back of the courtroom.

TIP: Expect that you will not be told which jail you are going to before you are transported to the jail.

TIP: It's a hard emotional experience, but try to remain as calm as you can.

TIP: When you are waiting to be transported to the jail you are going to, do not tell any other person what your conviction and sentence is.

Handcuffed, Shackled and Transported

After you are sentenced you will be placed in a holding cell until it's time for you to be transported to the jail you are going to. The guards will round you up from your cell. You will still be in the clothes that you wore in the sentencing trial. Any belongings you had (watch, ring, money etc.) will be placed in a bag and brought to the jail you are going to. You will be handcuffed and escorted to where the OPP transport vehicles are loaded. Prior to boarding you will be chained and handcuffed, and shackled with 5 or so other men. The OPP officers I experienced were not friendly, and the guys you are chained to aren't having a good day either. Don't draw any attention to yourself by being belligerent, crying, panicking, asking questions etc… Expect not to know which jail you are being brought to.

In the transport vehicle you will remain in handcuffs and be chained to a seat. In my case I was in protective custody, so I was in a separate secured area of the vehicle with several other men in protective custody.

Looking out the window you will see, when you arrive, the jail and the secured area, where they let you out. What you will see is hard core jail: fences, barbed wire, guards, concrete, and very cold looking. Intimidating and scary.

Yes, this whole process is emotionally and psychologically

draining and very intense. Hopefully you believe in God and silently pray that He will give you some peace and strength to hang in there.

TIP: **Remain calm. Don't panic or draw attention to yourself by asking questions, crying etc.**

TIP: **Prior to incarceration come up and stick with a safe reply (story) when asked what you 'are in for'. Examples include: 'I'm here to do my time', 'fraud', or 'I was set up and don't want to talk about it'.**

TIP: **Expect to start feeling more and more like a 'criminal' as you go through the transportation process.**

TIP: **Going in the 'prisoner' transportation vehicle will be intimidating and scary. Try to stay as calm as possible and do not speak with any other offenders travelling with you.**

TIP: **Expect to be disoriented as to where you are being taken to.**

JAIL LINGO

A&D

Admitting and Departure: an area in the jail where inmates are processed upon arrival, and when departing.

Blue shirt

Guards.

Bracelet

When you arrive in jail a bracelet is placed on with your prisoner ID number. The bracelet stays on you the entire duration of your sentence.

Canteen

Once a week you can order treats and supplies from the 'canteen' (a couple of guys come with bags of items ordered). Examples of items you can order are soft drinks, chips, candy, magazines, real coffee, protein powder, real tooth-paste, shower flip-flops...) you pay for the items from a bank account that holds the money you came in with, and/or family and/or friends send to the jail for you. There is a weekly limit to how much you can spend ($60 when I was in).

Celly

Cell mate.

Courtesy flush

When using the toilet in the cell for a bowel movement when your cellmate is present you are expected to flush the toilet before you are finished (half way through) to minimize the odor.

Count

Basically a roll call. The guard has a list of the men supposed to be on the range, and he/she calls out the names and each man has to say they are present.

Guardon the range

When a guard walks onto the range, one of the men will announce it so all the men are aware, and behave and act respectfully (or stop doing what they shouldn't be. Reasons for a guard coming on the range include checking cells, count, announcements, or escorting someone off the range.

General pop

General population are men who are not in protective custody. There are ranges that are general pop and ranges that are protective custody.

Hawk

Someone accused of being a hawk refers to a man who is trying to see another man's genitals when the person is showering.

Hole

Solitary confinement. Inmates who have caused trouble (fighting, stealing, death threats, violence, mental instability...) are placed in solitary confinement. From what I heard its purpose is to punish the inmate so that he will not cause trouble again. I've heard it can involve isolation, no bed, little or no time outside cell, and likely worse by guards (especially if the inmate assaulted a guard).

Home jail

The first jail you were placed in, even if temporarily.

Lock down

A time when you are locked in your cell, and not allowed out for the normal times. The length of lockdowns can be as short as a few hours, or can be weeks. The longest I experienced was about 2 weeks when I was in Penetanguishene. Reasons for lockdowns include: guards searching for a weapon, contraband, something stolen, investigating a fight, extracting someone who's at risk (or who caused a 'fight' (which they determine by watching surveillance footage), caused an incident. Most often it's because guards are working to rule, striking, or short staffed. For lock downs that stretch into days they allow men out one or two at a time for about a half hour to shower and make a phone call if they want. Visitors are not notified in advance, and when they show up for a visit they are usually turned away. Sometimes the lockdowns can be aggressive, with guards entering each cell one by one and tearing it apart, either looking for something in particular, or to confiscate things like extra clothing and materials used for purposes other than intended for. I experienced one lockdown where guards entered the range and cells in riot gear.

Meds up

This is when the nurse comes to the bars at the front of the range and dispenses meds through a slot in the bars. One or more men on the range will announce 'meds up' when they see nurse with her cart. This occurs 2x/day. Nurses are accompanied by a guard. They are on the other side of the bars, and dispense the meds through a slot.

Newby / First timer

Someone who has never been in jail before.

Offender

Someone convicted of a crime and sentenced to jail.

PC

Protective custody is for men whose lives are at risk, or who have committed a sexual offence – as a result their lives would be in danger if placed in a general pop range. It's also for men who would be in danger in a general pop range because there is someone, or some men who know them and would harm them. Lawyers will request PC for you, and sometimes judges order it.

Pack your shit

Guards use this phrase to tell you that you are being taken off the range. When they tell you this you have about 15 minutes from then to when your cell door is unlocked and you are escorted off the range. Reasons for being taken off the range include being transferred to another range or jail, and the best one is that you are being released after serving your time! If it's because you are being transferred to another jail they won't tell you where you are going. If you have too many things to carry (reading materials, parole papers, photos…), put them in a pillow case. Guards will inspect the items, and confiscate some at their discretion.

Range

Provincial jails are divided into contained and secure sections (ranges) where groups of inmates live. The vary in size and the number of men that live there, varying from about 10 – 20 in protective custody ranges, to 40+ in general ranges. In each range there are individual cells in which you will be assigned to live. In my experience there were two men to a cell, but I have heard and read that in some overcrowded jails there are 4 men to a cell. The cells are small (approximately 10ft by 11ft), with block walls on 3 sides, bars and a locked door at the front, and a concrete floor. The 'beds' are bunk style (top and bottom) constructed of either concrete or metal. I always chose the top bunk. It seems most other guys that were cell mates preferred the bottom. There are a stainless steel toilet and sink in the cell. There are also two small steel tables and chairs which are fixed in place.

Recreation time

The guards use this term to announce that you can go out to the 'exercise yard' if you want to. Usually twice a day, but not always, especially during lockdown.

Servers

In each range there are 2 'servers'. These are inmates living on the range who have been given the privilege, so to speak, of serving meals and supplies (bedding etc.) to men on the range. They also clean (if you can call it that) the common areas of the range. As 'payment' they receive extra food, and have extended free time on the range. My experience is that they are usually are men who have spent the longest time on the range, and are selected by guards because they are not trouble makers.

Super coup

Super coup is a higher security version of PC where the inmate is segregated (and safe) from any other inmates. It's for men whose life is in danger because it's known that there is a death threat.

White shirt

Guards ranked as supervisors (a few times I had to ask to see a white shirt). Blue shirt guards report to white shirt supervisors.

Yard

Secure area outside where you can get fresh air and walk or run a little.

Arrival at Jail – Processing

My experience with the Provincial jail system in Ontario was at Maplehurst Correctional Facility in Milton, the Penetanguishene 'super jail' in Penetanguishene, and the Lindsay super jail in Lindsay.

Maplehurst is a holding jail for those awaiting sentencing, and those that have been sentenced, and are waiting for placement at one of the jails in Ontario where 'offenders' go to serve their sentence. Prior to my legal problems I had driven by Maplehurst on many occasions, but had no idea what life was like for the inmates there.

The criminal lawyer I used for my defense had 'promised' me that the worst case scenario would be that I would receive a weekend sentence where you go in Friday night and come out Monday morning. The concept was that you could maintain employment during the week, and be with your family. He also added, "I don't want to see you go to Maplehurst because it's not a place fit for a dog." That statement ratcheted up my fear and anxiety when I was sent there.

Once you are allowed to exit the transport vehicle, you are led, again gang-handcuffed and shackled with other men, into the admitting part of the facility. The transport officers hand their manifest list over to the jail guards, and one by one you are allocated to holding cells to await processing. Expect these holding cells to be filthier than you can imagine.

You will likely get something to eat such as a sandwich and a bag of milk. You can also expect to be in the holding cell with other men of various ages and backgrounds, and with different offences and sentences.

TIP: **Expect and get used to filthy cells.**

TIP: **Remain calm. Expect it to take a long time, and that men will come and go from the holding cell. You may also be moved to other holding cells before it's your turn.**

TIP: **Don't initiate conversation, or make any prolonged eye contact.**

You will see men who have travelled through the jail system before, and know the routine. You will also see men who know each other. Some will be arrogant and cocky, and most will be pissed off. Surprisingly though, some will appear almost like they are coming home because they have been in and out so often. You don't want to stand out as a scared 'newbie', so just be (appear) as calm and quiet as you can.

TIP: **Stay quiet and calm. If someone talks to you, give a short answer (nothing specific about what you are in for).**

TIP: **Expect and get used to very foul language from inmates and guards.**

TIP: **Do not make prolonged eye contact with anyone, or stare at anything that stands out (tattoos, big, loud etc…).**

You will be able to see and hear the other holding cells being opened, and inmates called out by their last name.

When your turn arrives you will first be led, along with others, to a chair-like device that you sit in. I believe it's a metal detector to identify anyone with weapons in their rectum. You will then go to a room where a nurse (with a guard watching and listening) will ask you questions ("Do you have tattoos or markings? Are you on medications?") You will receive a tuberculosis shot, and be given a wrist band with your prisoner number on it. Then, you will be led to an area where you will take off your clothes. The area is one with kind of like pens, with waist high walls. The officers in this area I found to be particularly not happy (i.e. pissed off) with their jobs, and very rough and dominant over the inmates being processed.

Listen, and do what you are told. Expect foul language. After you take off your street clothes they will place them in a bag that you will receive when you are released. Any money you have will be placed into your account for 'canteen' – more on that later. So once you are naked they will tell you to open your mouth, then to raise arms up, then to turn around and bend over. In case you haven't figured it out, what they are looking for is concealed weapons and drugs. As you will hear stories during your jail time, people go to great lengths and danger to hide drugs, in particular in the body cavities. The anus is the preferred hiding place, and the second is swallowing condoms filled with drugs.

TIP: **Expect foul language and aggressive behavior from both inmates and guards.**

TIP: **Listen to guards' instructions, and do what they say.**

Back to the processing. After being searched you will be issued your jail attire which includes an orange jump suit, orange shirt, a pair of blue boxers, a pair of white socks, and canvas shoes. You will also receive a blanket, bed sheets, soap, toothbrush, toothpaste, and comb. These toiletries, if you can call them that, are cheap, disposable, and of poor quality.

After processing you will be led by guards to the range and cell you are assigned to. The jails I was in, especially the super jails, are large, so the walk may be longer than you expect.

As you will hear and discover, inmates have an unspoken pecking order of 'good' offences and 'bad' offences. The good get respect, and the bad are looked down upon, and can be the target of physical harm.

Regardless of what you are in for, never tell anyone what your crime is, and expect many to try and get you to tell them. If your conviction made the TV news or newspaper, there is a higher probability that some on your range will know what you are in for. Prior to going into the system, come up with a few lines to answer. Some options include 'I'm just in to do my time', or 'possession', or 'domestic'.

TIP: Expect to be asked many times by different men over the course of your sentence what you are in jail for.

TIP: Prior to going to jail come up with and practice a few brief words to answer the question as to why you are in jail. Examples include 'domestic', 'possession', 'fraud', 'I'm just here to do my time'.

Physical & Mental Health Problems in Jail

If you suffer from a physical or mental problem / illness you will not receive any preferential treatment. During my incarceration I saw men in wheelchairs, men suffering from serious illnesses and medical conditions, and many with mental illness. On my first day on the range, I heard someone say 'meds up', and then about 80% of the men lined up to get their medication dispensed to them by a nurse giving them through an opening in the bars at the front of the range. When I didn't line up, one of the men on the range asked if I wasn't going to 'get my meds', and was surprised that I wasn't taking any.

Sadly, most of those receiving mediation were suffering from mental illness. Jails have become a recycling place for people with mental illness who are not receiving proper care and support in their community. From my observation in the three jails I was in approximately 70% of the men I saw and interacted with had a mental illness.

Compounding this problem are factors such as:

- do not have supportive families

- struggle with addictions and relapse after release

- chronic unemployment

- no financial resources

- inadequate or no housing

- no, or inadequate therapy and counselling

- friends / acquaintances who are a bad influence

- no hope that their life will get better

Sadly, there are some people who plan to get arrested again and sent to jail during the cold months so that they have shelter and food.

If you are taking any medication, do not tell anyone what it is. There are certain medications that are 'traded'. How this works is that the person receiving the medication hides it in his mouth (the meds are given in a small paper cup and then the nurse and a guard make sure that it's swallowed. The person has to open their mouth, lift their tongue to show that they swallowed it. I don't know how they do it, but those trading their med go back and take it out of their mouth, then give it to the person they are trading with. From what I saw, the majority who have traded to receive it grind it up and then snort it. Trades are usually made for sought after food items (such as peanut butter), items from the weekly canteen, or protection.

TIP: **If you are on medication do not tell anyone what it is.**

TIP: **If you have a physical handicap or mental illnesses do not expect to get any sympathy or preferential treatment.**

TIP: **If you are on medication never trade it, or give it anyone.**

Jail Guards – Good, Bad & Very Ugly

The guards you encounter will either be good, bad (harsh, angry) or very ugly(cause physical harm). From my experience the good tend to be in short supply. The bad are the majority and the very ugly you will hear about from others on your range, and hopefully won't encounter. By bad I mean they act and talk tough and have zero patience with anyone not following the rules. Those that fall in the ugly category will have a reputation that precedes them.

Men who have committed a sex offence are at a higher risk with some guards in jails. Some may even announce what the offence is to others on the range, treat them more harshly, and even beat them up. I know one gentleman who was assaulted by two guards when he was going through the admitting process at Maplehurst. They purposely kept him as the last to be processed, and when the other men were gone they took him to an area where they knew surveillance cameras couldn't see, and then beat on him so much they knocked out a tooth, and caused bleeding. They threw a rag at him and told him to clean up his blood and not to tell anyone or they would hurt him more next time. Another man I know that went to Maplehurst was told by a guard that he wanted to cut his head off.

Some of the guards are 'white shirts', senior ranking

guards who have more authority over decisions, and they supervise non-white shirt guards. White shirts get involved when there is an issue, problem or request that falls outside the norm. From my experience it appears that if you ask for a white shirt, the other guards might get grumpy over the request, but they don't block the request. You may have to insist, and repeat the request.

During my stay there were three occasions where a white shirt got involved with me, and I have to say they were helpful and kind. The first was when I arrived at Maplehurst for the first time and wasn't initially placed in a PC (protective custody) range. Within a few minutes of being placed on a range, despite being a 'newbie' I sensed it wasn't a PC range. I appealed to the guard who took me out and placed me in a holding cell by myself. A white shirt sorted out that I was supposed to be in a PC range and he arranged for that to happen.

The second time was when I was being processed to be released from Lindsay. I had applied for and been granted that my parents would pick me up at release. It became obvious that the guards processing me were not aware I was approved to be picked up two weeks later, and were sending me towards admitting and departure, where I would be placed on a bus for transporting to my 'home jail'. I appealed to a guard that there was a mistake, and then when that wasn't going anywhere I asked to speak with a white shirt. He then took the time to look into my situation and confirmed that I could be released to my parents who were waiting.

The third time happened during the process of being released. Prior to release they return to you whatever clothes and personal items they had bagged when you first came into the system. This bag travels with you to wherever they send you, but you don't see it until you are released. You are supposed to receive back your 'street clothes'. It turns out they couldn't find my bag, and after about an hour or so delay while they searched, a white shirt got me and then took me to a room where I received used street clothes that they had in stock so to speak. A month after release they found my belongings and I had to drive back to pick them up.

TIP: Be low key and obedient with all guards during the release process

TIP: If necessary ask for a white shirt guard, if you know that something is happening, or will happen, which is a problem that blue shirt guards are doing nothing about. Examples include being threatened with physical harm, being placed in a general population range when you should be on a PC range, being shipped out for your release earlier than you are supposed to be.

TIP: No matter how long your clothes have been in that bag in storage you will be putting them on in the state they are in, so consider that when deciding what to wear to the sentencing trial.

TIP: Don't expect guards to be friendly, or sympathetic that it's your first time in jail.

LIFE ON THE RANGE

After this you will be led to a 'range' where you will be for your duration. Jails are divided into ranges where men are contained. There are 'general population' ranges, and 'protective custody' (also known as PC) ranges. General population ranges hold more men (about 36), than the PC ranges, which hold about 18.

In Ontario the ranges in the super jails are organized around an elevated central command centre so to speak. There are about 6 ranges per pod. The super jails house up to about 2,000 inmates. The PC ranges and general pop ranges are the same (size etc.) in each pod. Men in the general pop ranges can be close to the PC ranges, and are suspicious of men who are in a PC range. As a generalization, men in general pop ranges are rougher, and there are more fights and threats in general pop ranges.

From the command center guards monitor the ranges and men, and remotely control the door locks and lights etc. in the ranges, and in the corridors attached to the pod. Bars separate the ranges from the central area, and each range has a door from the range to the central area. Door locks for the range and individual cells are remotely controlled from the central area. There are corridors connected to the pods, and an outdoor secure 'exercise yard' off one of the corridors.

TIP: If you are supposed to be in a PC range, but end up in a general population range, don't hesitate to get a guard's attention to say you are supposed to be in PC. If you have to, say your life is in danger in general population.

TIP: When you arrive on a range for the first time it will take some time to get used to it (as much as one can get used to it). It feels and looks cold and hard core. It has a daily routine and rhythm that you will catch onto quickly.

At Penetanguishene and Lindsay I was initially placed in a temporary range, which is where inmates are placed until they are assigned the range that they will serve their time. These temporary ranges are a mixture of new inmates waiting placement, and inmates from other ranges who have been placed there as punishment, typically due to fighting. Tension and risk are higher in these temporary ranges.

TIP: Especially when you just arrive on a range, do not stand out; just quietly blend in.

TIP: The temporary ranges are a mixture of general pop men and PC men. Be very discerning and careful about whom you talk with.

TIP: Do not tell anyone if you are told in advance by a guard that you will be moving to another range.

Ranges have the cells on one end, and then there is a large common area with showers and a toilet, an area with tables, and an open area. Everything is concrete and steel. Expect your ass to be sore from sitting on concrete and steel all the time. The only showers in a range are those in the common area – shared by all inmates. They are somewhat private (you take clothes off and on and shower without anyone seeing your genitals unless they purposely look). The shower area is somewhat open on purpose so that guards can see whether that area is being used to beat up someone.

Each cell has a stainless steel toilet and sink, but during the times that you are locked out of your cells, you have to share the one common toilet on the range. The common toilet has half walls around it, so it's somewhat private. My observation and experience is that fellow inmates are respectful of each other's privacy during bathroom or shower use.

The three jails I was in (Maplehurst, Penetanguishene, and Lindsay) each had different rules as to when you have to come out of your cells, and when you have to go back in. The common schedule is that you come out after breakfast, then back in for lunch, out in the afternoon, in for dinner, and then out for a while before lockdown for the night.

If you are a newbie like I was, then you might experience firsthand what is meant by the term 'scared shitless'. The environment was so foreign, surreal and frightening that it was about a week before I could have a bowel movement. Fortunately, there are some unwritten codes of conduct for inmates. When you have to use the toilet in the cell, your cell mate will look the other way. If you are having a bowel movement you have to do a 'courtesy flush', i.e. flush before you are finished so the cell doesn't stink.

After a while you can get into a routine where you and your 'celly' (cell mate) take turns using the toilet in the cell when the cell doors are open.

TIP: **Look the other way when your cell mate is using the toilet**

TIP: **When having a bowel movement, flush the toilet about half way through**

Using the showers on the range takes some time to get used to. When you first arrive on a new range the protocol is to take a shower right away. If you don't take a shower right away you will be, at the least, harshly spoken to, and possibly assaulted. The only exception is if you arrive during lockdown, and are placed directly into a cell. In that scenario you take a shower first thing when you are let out.

There is communal shampoo in the showers, and you are given your own bars of soap. Seasoned inmates notice if anyone is not showering regularly (and they give that person a hard time), so taking a shower at least every other day is advisable.

TIP: **Get used to no privacy.**

TIP: **Shower right away when you arrive on a new range.**

TIP: **Shower regularly, at least every other day.**

TIP: **Get used to unsanitary conditions (examples: common toilet, dirty floors).**

On the days you take a shower you roll up your towel, place your bar of soap in it and then figure out the timing of taking a shower. If a shower is not being used, then you can go for it. If the showers are busy, then what the guys do is place their rolled up towel on the half wall near the shower. Then showers are taken in the order of the towels.

TIP: **Expect to have much more body odor than you usually have – I think it's due to a combination of the poor quality of the food, and stress.**

TIP: Don't stare or look longer than necessary at the shower being used, or you run the risk of being called a 'bird watcher'

Prison clothing consists of an orange overall, orange t-shirt, boxers, cotton socks, and slip- on canvas shoes with a really thin sole. My feet got sore walking on concrete until I bought some inserts through canteen. Each week you get a clean overall, a couple of clean shirts, boxers and socks. You also get clean bed sheets each week.

On each range there are one or two phones that you can call out (collect) on. Each range seems to have one or more phone hogs, who are first to use it, and often longer than most. Calling out to family was a life line to me, and by watching you can figure out a good time to have your turn, without someone trying to listen in.

TIP: Assume that phone conversations can be monitored and recorded.

TIP: Having someone to call is a great source of hope and encouragement.

You can only call out collect, and the person accepting the collect call gets charged exorbitant rates when they receive their bill. You will likely be approached and asked by men if you can let them use your call for a '3way'. I never said yes, and advise that you say no. I think it's a way for them to somehow use the line to call someone (without having to call collect, or pay).

After lockdown at night there is a period of time before lights go off for the night. Actually they don't go off; they are just dimmed. Guys use this time either to lie down, read, talk, etc... Whenever you are locked in your cell, day or night, a guard will come around once every hour and look into your cell.

TIP: **Don't sleep during the day, so you can sleep better at night.**

You will notice that in whatever jail you go to there are men who have been in and out of jail so often that they are comfortable with it, know other inmates, know guards. Some almost seem happy to be there. Sadly there are those who have no family or support on the outside, or even adequate shelter and food, so they end up being recycled back in.

You will also notice that there are an unusually high percentage of men who are on medication, the majority of whom have a mental illness.

Three meals a day are 'served' to you when you are locked in your cell (except at Penetanguishene, where it's served while you are out on the range). There is a slot in the cell door through which a tray of 'food' is given to you by 'servers'.

Some inmates seem to like the food. Personally, I found it quite disgusting. The trays have a plastic seal on them, so that gives some comfort that it's not contaminated with surprises. Drinks (milk, orange juice) are in plastic bags which you pierce with a straw, or cut open with your teeth. Cutlery is plastic, and there is no plate. You get a Styrofoam cup. Servers come around with a beverage container from which you can get hot water for either tea or coffee.

If you like bread, you will be happy because lots of bread is included with the meals. The different types of meals cycle through, so to some extent you get variety each day. Some of the meals are referred to by nicknames such as 'chicken guts', 'donkey dinks'... In a chicken guts meal I once saw a chicken heart, so the title is aptly named.

Some men put on a lot of weight in jail (eating lots of bread). Personally I went in at 180lbs and a 36" waste, and came out at 132lbs with a 31" inch waste.

There is a way to get better quality food. You can say you are a vegetarian, or on a low sodium diet, or no lactose diet, or eat only kosher food. With vegetarian meals you get more peanut butter, for example.

TIP: **Consider requesting a special diet to get better quality food. Make the request with the nurse at intake, and/ or by using the request form on the range.**

There are two 'servers' on each range. Servers are fellow inmates who live on that range. They typically will have been there among the longest, and the guards have selected them for that role. In addition to serving, they 'clean' the range common area and distribute toiletries, bedding, changes of clothes. In some jails, however, as at Lindsay, the toiletries and bedding are left on a table in the range and then it's a free for all.

Servers get 'paid' with extra free time on the range when everyone else is locked in, and they also get some extra food. In addition to being a server, there are other 'jobs' you can 'apply to'. Jobs include working in the kitchen or the laundry. You apply by expressing interest to the guards, and/or writing it down on a request form. Only inmates in good standing with the guards get these jobs.

TIP: **Be kind and polite with your servers.**

In jail you can have a 'bank account' where money can be deposited by a loved one or friend. You then can use that money to purchase 'canteen' items. Once a week you can fill out an order form for canteen items. Examples of available items include peanut butter, real coffee, protein powder, healthy snacks, unhealthy snacks, quality toiletries, reading materials, games, etc… There is a dollar limit as to how much you can spend each week ($60 when I was in).

Canteen is the reason I recommend having money in your pocket when you go to the sentencing hearing, so that you have some money in your 'bank account' to pay for the canteen.

TIP: **Have money in your pocket at your sentencing trial, and/or arrange for a loved one to send money which will be placed in your bank account.**

If you are so blessed, canteen is a great treat to look forward to. Also, by selectively sharing something with your celly (or someone else) you will build a friendship. Also, some inmates trade canteen items. Occasionally peanut butter is provided with your meals, and it's a 'valuable' item which some men will trade in exchange for other canteen items.

TIP: **It's okay to say no when someone asks you to trade. Be selective aboutwith whom, what, and how often you trade.**

There will be some men who sadly do not have any money, and therefore cannot buy from the canteen. There are acts of kindness and friendship between men. I often saw men without be given something from men who have, and even sometimes asking others whether they would like something in particular from the canteen. In my case, I had a celly at Penetanguishene who never received money to purchase canteen items, so I shared with him.

Some also play poker using canteen items as money. I

caution against that, as I've seen it cause arguments, and in one case an inmate went into canteen debt so to speak, and had to be pulled off the range for his safety.

There is a process in the jails where you submit requests to the guards. There are request forms and a box at the front of the range. Only guards can open the box and retrieve the requests. Sometimes your request will be answered, and sometimes not. Examples of requests include: see a doctor, request sleeping medication, or request to be a server or to work in kitchen).

TIP: You may have to submit the same requests more than once, if you don't get a reply. Don't expect all requests to be granted.

TIP: Food and especially treats from the weekly canteen are like money when you are in jail. Selectively trading with other fellow inmates can foster good relationships. Occasionally give your celly a treat. It will help you get along with each other, and your celly might be more motivated to stand up for you if you are being harassed by other inmates.

TIP: Find out about programs that are available for you to sign up for. They can be a great way to help pass time, and give you something to look forward to.

How to Avoid Getting the Shit Kicked Out of You

Most guys just want to do their time and get out without any incidents or problems. There are, however, usually several trouble-makers on a range.

Following are some guidelines as to what you should and should not do, in order to stay safe:

- Assume everyone lies – about what and how long they are in for, and about why they are asking you questions.

- Be cautious with men who seem like they want to be friends. My experience was that the few men I was friends with did not ask what I was in for. I believe God brings people into our lives at the right time, and that was my case in being able to discern with whom I could be friends. Once you are comfortable with the person(s), it's healthy to have someone to sit and talk with.

- No whistling. Ranges are like a cage, and for some reason in prison culture there is no whistling among inmates because it infers men are birds in a cage.

- Don't touch other inmates' stuff.

- Don't steal.

- Don't stare at others, or make prolonged eye contact – even if they are staring at you often.

- If it's meal time and you are in a jail where men eat at tables in the range common area, and you are going to sit at a table with one or more men already there, ask first if the seat is taken.

- Don't flush the toilet between lights out and lights on hours (toilets used at night are covered with a used towel or boxers).

- When using the shower change in and out of your clothes discretely, and if others are waiting to use the shower don't stay in too long.

- Don't be loud or aggressive.

- Don't mouth off to others or call them names.

- Don't gossip.

- Don't 'rat out' on anyone (for example, if there is a fight, don't say who started it, or who was involved).

- If a fight breaks out, and you are close, move out of the way quickly. Some fights I saw make UFC fighting look like sandbox play. Some men fight to do serious harm and even to kill.

- You will see men pass notes between ranges (when guards aren't looking). Do not get involved or talk about it.

- A pissed off guard might ask you within hearing range of other men, "What are you in for first timer?" Try to avoid answering as he/she is trying to get you in trouble with other men on the range. (Guards know, of course, what you are in for).

- Maintain a positive and respectful relationship with guards, and comply with what they ask/say.

- Wait your turn for showers and shaving. At Maplehurst you shave and cut your nails in the common washroom area where there are multiple sinks. At other jails (like ones I was in) you shave and cut nails in your cell. The razors are cheap, and often nick. Nail clippers are shared with all men on the range. The way it works is a guard comes around with the clippers in a liquid similar looking to what barbers use.

- Let your cell mate choose whether he wants the upper or lower bunk.

- Food is more valuable than money, and you can use it to gain favour and protection. Be on guard though that you don't get muscled (pressured) into giving away more than you still need to be nourished. Some guys can't get enough bread, for example, whereas I gave most of mine away. Also, peanut butter is considered one of the most valuable and desirable trades. Protein powder from canteen is up there as well.

- Giving your celly a treat from your food or canteen can help build a positive relationship, especially with a new cell mate, or if you are new to the cell.

Changes on the Range – Get Used to It

Life on the range includes men leaving and new men coming in. This is a point of stress, as you wonder who is coming in and whether they will be a trouble maker, or worse yet a personal safety concern, especially more so with new cell mates. If you are blessed with a good celly that you get along with, and yes in some cases even become friends with, you will find it disappointing when he leaves (and you don't).

My observation was some new guys coming on a range who are trouble-makers will act tough and maybe even stir things up, but eventually things settle down. Serious trouble- makers are usually dealt with quickly by other more dominant men on the range, or guards in instances where they instigate a fight. As far as new cell mates are concerned, my experience is that they try to match up compatible cell mates.

TIP: **During your time you will have different cellys – get used to it.**

TIP: **When you get a new celly, or you are a new celly to someone, take it easy and slow in getting to know each other.**

TIP: If your celly has been there for a while, observe how he interacts with other men on the range (whether he's respected, left alone, is friends with trouble makers, or is the subject of bullying).

TIP: Assume that no one tells the truth, especially regarding their story.

TIP: Assume everyone wants to find out what you are in for.

TIP: Do not stare at anyone on the range, even if they are looking at you.

TIP: If you feel you are in imminent danger from your celly, find a way to speak with a guard and tell him/her. My observation is that they take that seriously and will remove one of you off the range.

I was surprised at how many times men knew each other, and were happy to see each other. It's a sad reflection on how broken the system is with 'offenders' repeatedly going in and out of jail.

Creative Use of Materials

You will see some very unique and ingenious use of the limited materials available to inmates. At first I found them odd and of questionable use, but you will find it helpful to use some of them.

The ones I'm aware of include:

- Using a plastic pop bottle to fill up with hot water before evening lockdown to place under your blankets if it's winter and your cell is cold – which it is.

- Using chip bags to keep bread fresh (and to give to other men).

- Turning chip bags inside out to use as a mirror for holding outside bars to see TV.

- Using plastic pop bottles, which you can get by ordering pop from canteen, to mix and drink coffee or tea in.

- Using supplied toothpaste as glue (yes, seriously) to put up notes or whatever. I used it at night to stick a cover over the ventilation grill which blew out cold air.

- Using a string from a blanket to cut bagels.

- Using a strip of clothing or bedding for a clothes line.

- Using razors supplied for shaving to cut hair.

- Using sheets as a fishing rod to pass items between cells when locked in.

- Using plastic drink bags filled with water and wrapped in shirts as weights.

- Placing shoes upside down on toilet seat so there is no contact with your skin and the toilet seat.

- At night placing underwear (boxer shorts) stretched over toilet to keep sound and any odor out.

- Using extra clothes as a pillow.

- Making alcohol out of banana peels.

- Making tobacco out of banana peels.

- Making cigarette rolling paper from Bible pages. (Please don't).

- Washing clothes in shower for extra changes of clothes within the once/week supply, and to wear layers in winter months.

Doing Time, Passing Time

Spending time in jail and passing time in jail is hard, very hard, especially as a first timer. However, it is not impossible and it does not have to be such a disturbing experience that it breaks you. One comfort is that there is a predictable and reliable rhythm to time in jail. Sleep and wake time, meals, and free time are the same each day. Somewhat ironically, this helps you pass time, as you know what to expect next, and each of these regular daily things helps to pass time, and yes, gives you something to look forward to.

Following, in order of priority is what worked for me to do time / pass time:

- Pray, pray, pray.

- Bible reading / study / meditation.

- Listen for God.

- Stay connected with loved ones and friends on the outside by calls, letters, visits.

- Read any Christian material on the range.

- Sleep at night, not during the day.

- Keep moving (i.e. exercise) – walk the range, pushups, etc…

- Hopefully get visitors.

- Write letters.

- Make phone calls.

- If possible (i.e. if God blesses you) develop a friendship with someone you can relate to, trust, and share encouragement with.

- Take programs and courses available in the jails.

- If you like playing cards, you will be able to do that, every day if you want to.

- Think about the things you would like to do when you get released, but only if it doesn't make you depressed.

- Remember that no matter how long your sentence is, the day of your release will happen.

As a Christian I believe that Jesus is in control of everything, and everything passes through his hands before it happens. He either allows it to happen, or brings it to pass so that He can accomplish His perfect plan for our lives. As well, God uses all things for good – in His perfect timing and provision. In many instances, such as being in jail, it's impossible to see or figure out how He can use it for good. As time passes by, many years in my case, you will be able to look in the rear view mirror and see this principle working in your life.

Unless you are already a strong believer this is a hard truth to grasp, especially when you are sitting in a jail cell. At the time of writing this it has been 6 years since my release from incarceration. Looking in the rear view mirror, I can now see that God has used, and is still using that dark and painful period of my life for good.

I have guided and assisted several men I could not have

helped without my experience with the jail system. One was contemplating suicide, and another had a mental illness and was facing jail time.

In my experience, surviving incarceration, and coming out stronger and better, cannot be achieved without believing in and drawing closer to God. Prayer is the most powerful thing you can do in any circumstance. Trusting God to answer prayer is what faith is all about. Faith is trusting that He will answer those prayers that are in line with His will and promises in the Bible (spoken word of God), and in His perfect timing and provision. God's miracles are never early, never late. Often we have to wait and persevere for a long time. For myself, I have prayers that I've been praying for years.

Praying yourself, and having others on the outside pray for you, is the most valuable thing you can do.

While incarnated you will find it difficult to find healthy activities that will help you pass the time. In my case, and I believe for many others, God used my sentence and jail time to not only correct my illegal path, but to bless me with an abundance of time, and a hunger to learn about and study the Bible. If you open up your heart to God in genuine humility and repentance, He will answer you and guide you one step at a time.

No matter how long your sentence, never lose sight that you will be released one day. It's important to have things to look forward to after release. Staying connected to your loved ones and friends on the outside is very important. It takes your mind off the monotony of jail, and helps you feel that you are not abandoned. In addition to phone calls and visits, you can also write and receive letters.

TIP: Be aware when talking on the phone that nosy inmates try to hear what you are talking about. Also assume that the guards can listen in, if they want to.

TIP: Let those you are calling, and those visiting you know that lockdowns happen, and if they haven't heard from you, that is likely the reason. Those visiting may arrive on some visiting day only to find out it's in lockdown and there are no visits allowed, which is terribly frustrating, especially when they have driven a long way. They should call ahead on the day of visiting to confirm visiting hours.

TIP: Mail is opened, so whoever is sending you mail needs to be aware of that. Nothing extra can be sent to you with any letter they may send.

Having your loved ones and friends visit you is something special to look forward to, and helps you stay aware that there is hope and a life waiting for you upon release. Visitors need to contact the institution you are in to find out what the visiting hours and rules are. Some jails may require checking out visitors' backgrounds before they visit you. Visitors should show up a half hour before visiting time to allow for processing, and for the guards to bring you to the visiting.

The way it works for you, is that a guard will come onto the range and say your last name (e.g. Smith) visitor! A guard, and sometimes two, will escort you to the visiting room. Then after the visit, they will lead you back to your range and cell.

TIP: Visitors, especially first time, should expect dealing with a difficult process as well as guards that sometimes are not friendly. There are exceptions, but not in my family's experience.

The visiting room is divided, with inmates on one side, and visitors on the other. There are glass and a wall separating you. There are a number of chairs on both sides. There is a phone that you use to talk with each other. The way it works is that you wait for a spot to open up, then your visitors go to the open one. There is a 15 minute time limit, and then the guards turn the phone off and you have to leave. There is no opening in the glass partition so nothing can be passed to you, so there is no touching, hugging etc. Visitors can show you things on paper, pictures, and other objects.

TIP: Visitors experiencing their first visit to a jail can expect to be emotionally impacted by how hard core jail is. As well, when they see you for the first time in prison clothes it might be emotional for them.

In addition to requesting a Bible, you may come across Christian literature on your range. I suggest you read them. Christians often connect in jail by noticing that you are reading a Bible, and Christian literature. For myself, the Bible and Christian literature were life changing blessings, and were the starting point and desire to participate in Bible study.

I also found that men who were trouble makers left me alone after they saw me reading the Bible and Christian literature on the range. You can request a Bible. Bibles are made available in prisons by the wonderful ministries of The Gideons and the Salvation Army. My first Bible is the one I received in jail, and I took out with me.

TIP: When released you are able to take with you the possessions that you accumulated during your time. Examples are reading materials, and items obtained through canteen.

TIP: Reading is a good way to pass time. There will be reading materials on the range, and in some jails a librarian will come around with a book cart that you can sign out books.

TIP: Most jails have Christian literature, which for me really helped.

TIP: Request a Bible, read it, and study it. God will speak to you through it.

TIP: You can also order magazines from the weekly canteen.

Transferred to Different Jail(s)

In my case, after I was sentenced and sent to Maplehurst jail, I waited there to be sent to the jail where I would serve the sentence. It can take weeks or months before you are shipped out. They will not tell you when you will be shipped out, other than saying something like "in the next 4 days to two weeks."

Being shipped out happens after lockdown (everyone in their locked cells). You will hear your cell lock open (the locks are controlled remotely by guards), and then a guard will show up and tell you to 'pack up your shit and be ready in five minutes).

I was transferred twice, once from Milton to Penetanguishene, and then from Penetanguishene to Lindsay. The transfer to Lindsay came as a complete, unexpected surprise and they would not tell me where I was going. Being transferred is stressful, especially for the first time.

Being processed when you leave your current jail, and when you arrive at the new one involves new guards and inmates, new sights and sounds and unknowns. The big ones are who will be on the range you are assigned to, and who you will be sharing a cell with.

Note: Your family, loved ones, or friends are not notified
      of your transfer. They have to wait either until you

can call them from wherever you are transferred to, or they can call the jail you were at to inquire. It can happen then, that they show up for a scheduled visit, only to find out you are not there.

TIP: **You are not in control, so just relax and go with the flow.**

TIP: **Listen to guards' instructions.**

TIP: **Pray.**

TIP: **Remember the rules for when arriving on a new range, especially showering right away.**

TIP: **Remind your loved ones that you could be transferred, and it could take a few days before you can tell them where you are.**

TIP: **Don't assume the worst case; the next jail you are going to could be better.**

TIP: **Don't be surprised if the guards do not tell you which jail you are being transferred to.**

Working Jail

By a God orchestrated miracle I finished my sentence at the Lindsay super jail, which is a 'working jail'. At this type of jail there are opportunities to work in the tailor shops (sowing prison clothing), metal fabricating shop (making metal park benches and garbage cans), and the license plate shop. Shortly after arriving I was invited to be considered / interviewed for a 'job' (unpaid). The process consists of being interviewed by a psychiatrist, and then a panel of men or women who decide where you should be given a job, and if yes, where.

TIP: Good behavior is a must to be considered for a work placement.

From my observation, they do a good job at selecting men for the various jobs by personality type, age, and physical build, and they also consider whether you request a particular job. My celly had been working in one of the two tailor shops, and suggested that I request to work in one. Within a few days of the interview, I was blessed with being placed to work in Tailor Shop 'A'. Being able to work really helps time to pass, and gives you a purpose.

There are some benefits that come along with working. When you are working you get a morning and afternoon snack (usually cookies), and lunch is brought into the workshop where you sit at tables and eat with other men.

Sometimes the lunches are better than what's served on the range.

The working shops at Lindsay are about a five minute walk from the range. There is a strip and search checkpoint going and coming. You are not handcuffed, but you are escorted by guards and/or the civilians running the workshops. In the morning they call men out one man at a time for one workplace at a time. You line up and wait for all coworkers to be present, then everyone is patted down, and pockets checked. At the checkpoint, before entering the workshop, you go into stalls, so to speak, one by one, and have to remove your clothes. The routine is to stand, then arms up, then mouth open, then turn around and bend over.

TIP: **Expect to feel humiliated and vulnerable during the strip and search.**

Upon arriving at the new range for working inmates I was placed in a cell with a celly named 'Harold'. My observation is they do a pretty good job at Lindsay of matching cellmates (age, personality, working same shop). At this point in my journey I brought with me a Bible and some other Christian materials. Harold noticed these, and he had some identical materials. He invited me to participate in a Bible study group of fellow believers among the inmates.

This Bible study group met on the range concrete floor, each night before lock down. There were on average about six to ten of us who met for about a half hour or so. Occasionally other men would mock us or try to disrupt us, but for the most part they left us alone. This range was the only range from the prison population of 2,500 that had believers who met each night for Bible Study! A miracle.

TIP: There are no coincidences in life – God is in control of everything all the time, even though things may feel completely out of control.

TIP: If there is more than one 'job' opportunity go for the one that suits your physical abilities.

TIP: Getting a job will help you feel normal so to speak.

TIP: Keep an eye out for anyone in your working shift that could be a trouble maker and if they are don't interact with them.

TIP: Work hard, and do a good job. It will gain you favour with whoever is supervising you.

Trying for Parole

In Ontario you can apply for parole (early release) after serving one third of your sentence. You have to go through an application process, involving paperwork, and an interview with a staff person who handles and coordinates it. It also includes knowing whoever you would be living with, if parole is granted, being interviewed, a police background check, and visiting the location where you would be living.

If your application passes the prescreening stage, then you get scheduled for a parole board hearing. It's held in a room at the jail and you are present with whoever you would be living with if granted parole. The board consists of a 3 member panel. Basically they ask you a lot of questions to see if they think you are eligible. You can expect that they will ask about whether you have taken responsibility, what you have done to deal with your issue (for example counselling), and why you think you will not reoffend. The probability of getting parole is very low, particularly for certain classes of offences, such as murder, sex offences.

TIP: **Do not get your hopes up for early release, because it can be very depressing, especially for a first timer and their family, if you don't get it. I've heard that the number of offenders paroled is kept very low in order to keep the jails full.**

TIP: Do not tell anyone on the range that you are applying for parole. There can be men on the range who have no chance of parole, and who are serving a long sentence. Out of jealousy they will try to ruin someone's opportunity for parole, by trying, for example, to draw them into a fight.

Parole conditions are stricter than probation conditions, so you want to make sure that you are capable of fulfilling the conditions. The conditions include weekly reporting to your parole officer, and basically house arrest with some limited provision to go out for such things as medical appointments. It also could involve wearing an electronic monitoring device around your ankle so they can tell if you leave where you are living. A breech of any of the parole conditions sends you back to jail quickly, and with a longer sentence.

TIP: As much as possible, keep your parole paperwork hidden in your cell. There are not many options, so I placed mine under my mattress.

TIP: Expect to be grilled by the parole board members that are interviewing you.

TIP: Rehearse in your mind how you will answer questions like, why should you be granted parole, or what have you done to make sure you won't reoffend.

Preparing for Release

In Ontario you can be released early, after serving two thirds of your time, if you have had no incidents (bad behavior, fighting, etc.) while you were doing your time. A coordinator will contact you in advance to let you know the date. If you have someone who will pick you up, you have to give the coordinator information about who the person(s) is/are so they can be confirmed and approved.

If there will be no one picking you up, then you will shipped back to your 'home jail' before your release date. This could be a few days to a week before. From my experience, and from what I have heard, it's best to have someone pick you up if possible. Getting shipped out to your home jail for a short time (days to a couple of weeks) has its associated stressors.

To state the obvious, the jail system is far from perfect, and mistakes happen. In my case I was called out for release processing a week before I was scheduled to be picked up by family. Despite protesting, I was taken to A and D (admitting and departure) where I had to ask for a white shirt and explain that I was approved to be released a week later to family. It took about an hour to confirm that this was correct.

Before release you are supposed to be given your street clothes and belongings to change into and take with you. They couldn't find my bag, despite trying for an hour or so.

Finally, they gave me some clothes to put on. My family was stressed, of course, wondering what was taking so long.

Some weeks later they found my clothes, and I had to drive back to retrieve them.

TIP: Do not tell anyone on the range what your release date is. Some men who are in for a long time, or are trouble makers will try to have the person being released get into a fight (which would cancel their release and keep them in for their full sentence length). Also, it seems to be a 'tradition' that the person being released gets put in the shower with his clothes on – either voluntarily or involuntarily.

TIP: Whoever is picking you up should not be concerned if you are released later than the scheduled time.

TIP: Decide before your release what you are taking with you and what are you leaving behind. Consider giving items you don't need to your celly or someone else you became friends with. It's an act of kindness that could make a positive difference for them.

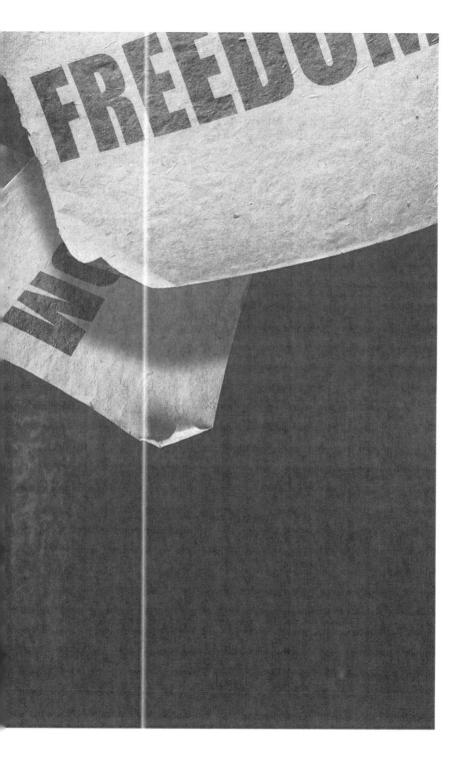

FREEDOM!

While the time I served was relatively short compared to countless others, I briefly felt almost guilty about leaving when others that you had lived with and become friends with were remaining to endure the remainder of their sentence. It is good during time served to see men being released – it gives you a sense of hope that one day your release will happen.

The dark, evil side of the system had a departing shot at me just before I walked out into freedom. The last guard that I interacted with before walking out said, "make sure you come back soon so I can have job security". This was a sad example of those prison guards who do more harm than good.

Walking out of the prison (hell) into freedom is both joyful and a huge stress relief. The freedom, fresh air, seeing and hugging loved ones, experiencing the real 'normal world' and eating real food are all glorious gifts. Gifts that I previously took for granted.

Freedom never felt that good, and food never tasted better.

Prison time labels you as an offender (i.e. a criminal), and this is a hard feeling to get rid of. For me, it's taken a long time, and for months after my release I felt like I was walking around with something visibly different that people would see, and know that I had served time in jail. This feeling was largely due to the shame of my offence and my sentence being purposely published in the media.

TIP: Do not be surprised if you feel a sense of guilt or sadness when being released. The longer your sentence, the more you may feel this way.

TIP: Enjoy, savour and give thanks for everything you have not been able to experience –family and friends, food, walking outdoors, comfortable bed, etc…

TIP: Depending on your crime, and any feeling of guilt or shame you have, you may experience a period where you feel paranoid about people treating you differently.

TIP: Depending on how long you have been in jail you can expect to have some culture shock as you get used to a normal life again.

Probation –
A Test of Patience

In Ontario most sentences carry a requirement that you are on Probation. The longest probation term you can receive is 3 years, which is what I received. Probation involves reporting after release to a probation officer at a probation office closest to where you reside. In my case I was required to report twice a month in person. Depending on your probation officer and your relationship with him or her, you might get a break and eventually have to attend once a month in person, then a call-in for the second.

The purpose of probation is to keep you on a short leash so to speak, to ensure you are abiding by your probation conditions, and to reduce the potential for reoffending. Apparently, as well, it's to support and guide you as you get your life back together. My experience was with a probation officer who was 'by the book', tough, discouraging, and initially came across like I would breach my probation conditions and end up being sent back to jail. In some cases you may need to provide proof of complying with a particular condition, for example that you are engaged in required counselling.

TIP: Make sure you clearly understand your probation conditions. Ask the probation officer to give examples of what would constitute a breach. Some are obvious, such as not showing up for a probation appointment. Some need discussion and explanation. For example, if you are prohibited from having any contact with someone, what happens if you see them in a shopping mall and they start talking to you?

TIP: You can request approval to have someone (for example, a parent) attend the probation meetings with you, if you have valid reason. For example, if you have a mental illness that makes it difficult to understand and remember what the probation officer says, then someone should accompany you.

TIP: It is possible to request and receive a variance to a probation condition. For example, you may have a condition that you cannot use a computer, but you obtain employment that requires you to use a computer. If the probation officer supports your variance request, then they will ask the prosecution whether they have an objection. If not, the probation officer will issue a formal variance, which, however, could have additional conditions which put parameters around the variance.

Although that was my experience, I've heard of other men who have had a very positive and helpful probation officer. Like any other service, the individual you are dealing with can have either a positive or negative influence on your interaction/relationship. A friend of mine, who served 2 years, and then 3 years' probation, developed such a positive relationship with his probation officer that they developed a friendship that extended to his family.

In my case, the relationship improved slowly and especially during the third year. However, I still had to go every two weeks to report at the probation office, and every time she would go over all of my probation conditions, asking me whether I had breached any of the conditions. Sometimes she would seem interested in talking about 'normal' things, but then unexpectedly throw in a blunt question of whether I was complying with a specific condition.

God had a purpose, though, for the probation officer I was assigned to. During one of the initial meetings she said, "So you've destroyed your life, your marriage, any relationship with your children, your job, your reputation, and you have no money. What are you going to do?" She also said, "You might as well accept that you'll just be able to get a job in a factory."

I responded by saying that through a miraculous experience in jail I had become a born again Christian, and started my day with the Bible and God.

She then gave me a pamphlet about a program called *Celebrate Recovery* that was run at a local Church. Unbeknownst to me, the leaders of that program had recently made a presentation to the probation officers about the program. As you will read later, I attended that program, which became instrumental in my recovery journey.

As tedious and frustrating as probation can be, it eventually comes to an end, and that chapter of your sentence is closed.

How to Avoid Reoffending / Relapse

I am certainly no expert, and the comments and advice in this book are based on the reasons that I ended up in jail, the reading and counselling I've done, the support groups that I've participated in and led as a facilitator, and most importantly God's miracle working power.

Just saying, "I won't do it again", does not cut it, is stupid, and is an indicator that you are in denial of the reason(s) you got arrested and sentenced in the first place. A game plan to avoid reoffending varies of course, depending on why you were charged and sentenced. Your individualized game plan will evolve over time, so don't stress about having it 100% figured out and in place prior to release. Don't make the mistake of trying to go it on your own with no help or support.

This is what my game plan looked like:

- Praying for God's help, and trusting that He knows what is best for me and will provide.

- Daily time with God (Bible reading, prayer, quiet time).

- Staying with supportive family.

- Regular Church attendance.

- Vigorous regular exercise program.

- Healthy eating.

- Getting enough sleep.

- Staying busy.

- 3 years' probation.

- Taking daily medication to address my Bipolar mental illness.

- 2 years of a specialized group program attended by men with similar reasons for being convicted.

- 2 years of Christian counselling.

- 4 years of attending *Celebrate Recovery*, including completion of a 12 step program and then facilitating a group for men with similar struggles.

- Only healthy friendships.

- Avoiding places, people, substances, sights, computers or whatever might trigger a relapse.

- Regularly meeting with an accountability partner with whom I could be totally real and honest.

- Moving forward (at first barely) no matter what, and not quitting.

Avoiding relapse and reoffending can be very difficult for some people, and can even be a struggle for years. In particular, if your problem is an addiction (drugs, alcohol, sexual addiction) you need to be prepared to deal with the temptations to use again. No one can beat an addiction on their own. Don't make the mistake of thinking that you can. If you relapse, no matter how many times, pick yourself up and keep going forward one day at a time. If you are a Christian, ask for and receive God's forgiveness.

The Miracle of God Revealing Himself to Me in Jail

Prior to being sentenced and incarcerated I knew that God was real, I prayed sometimes, and sometimes attended Sunday service at Churches. I was raised a Catholic, but didn't have a relationship with God (Jesus) until through a miraculous series of events God revealed himself to me, and gave me a choice.

When I was arrested and going through the legal process everyone who I thought were my 'friends' turned their back on me, with the exception of my good friend. He suggested I pray this prayer that he prayed personally, and as well it has helped members of his family going through difficult times.

'God is the source of my strength in whom I trust, therefore I will not fear'

I prayed this prayer infrequently at first, and then with increasing frequency. Over the years of praying it I got an image of my mind of a white cross. It was very faint at first, and then over time with continued prayer it became more visible to the point where I saw that it was white, and a certain size. Prior to being sentenced the image was quite clear in my mind, and I also had the impression of kneeling down on one knee and holding the white cross and it was protecting me.

I was sentenced and sent to Maplehurst. I was very scared and depressed. When I was processed a guard escorted me to a range. As soon as the bars closed behind me and I looked around something inside me said this is not PC, get out. I caught the guard's attention, and told him I was supposed to be in PC. He took me off the range and said he was not informed of that. He asked me if I felt my life was in danger. I said yes, and he placed me in a temporary holding cell, and then conformed I was supposed to be in PC.

I was then brought to a PC range. It was evening, so men were in their locked cells. I was placed in one with one man there already. The upper bunk was open, and I climbed up. By this point I was at my rock bottom. I seriously thought about how I could kill myself, thinking I couldn't last one day, yet alone my entire sentence.

I was sitting on the bunk completely defeated and lost, when I looked at the block wall at the foot of my bunk. It was painted white, and someone before me had outlined in pencil the shape of a cross – the same size cross I had seen in my mind, when I had been praying the prayer that my friend had given me. Overwhelmed with the experience I flopped back on my bed and looked up at the concrete ceiling which you can reach with your hands from the bunk. There were years of writing and scribbles on the ceiling from men who had previously occupied the upper bunk in that cell. As I stared at the ceiling one kind of floated and captured my attention- 'Trust God and He will help you'.

At that moment I knew that God had placed me in that cell at that time, and that He was giving me a choice – His way, or my way. PTL (Praise the Lord) I made a decision then to choose His way.

Faith and the Spiritual Battle

This is my faith journey to Christianity, and being arrested and incarcerated was what God used to open my heart to who He is.

I now know and believe that nothing is by random or chance.

God is always in control and uses all things for good.

I believe that God is always in control of our lives, and has a good plan for everyone regardless of our mistakes (sins). I did not always know and completely believe this truth until God moved in my life.

Having hope (even just a glimmer), patience, encouragement and support are important for the rebuilding of your life. Becoming a Christian gave me that and more.

When I accepted Jesus Christ into my heart, and accepted the free gift of salvation, all of my sins were forgiven and I became a new person in Christ. This is available to everyone. If you are not at that point, or don't believe, or are of a different faith, you may wish to consider and explore whether it's true.

The spiritual battle is real (evil vs. good), more real than this world.

Satan and his demons are very present and active in the jail system, and throughout the world. Jesus won victory over Satan, and because I accepted Jesus I believe that I was protected in the jails I was in, and He has blessed me in incredible ways since.

Need for Change in the Prison System

The statistics of the Canadian prison population are grim.

- One in five inmates is over age 50

- The average level of education is Grade 8

- 80% of offenders have addiction or substance abuse problems

- 31% have Hepatitis C and 5% have HIV

- Almost half of all offenders require mental health care

- The rate of incarceration of aboriginal women increased by 80 per cent in the past decade

- The number of visible minorities in Canadian prisons has increased by 75 per cent in the past decade

- It costs an average of $110,000 a year to house a male inmate

Thank you for reading this book. I pray that God will bless you, protect you, and answer your prayers.

To order additional copies of this book go to www.survivingjail.ca.

CPSIA information can be obtained at www.ICGtesting.com
Printed in the USA
LVOW10s0418090316

478332LV00010B/53/P

9 780993 821370